COOL CAREERS
WITHOUT COLLEGE
FOR PEOPLE WHO LOVE TO
REPAIR THINGS

MARCIA AMIDON LUSTED

ROSEN
PUBLISHING®

New York

To my husband Greg, who can fix anything

Published in 2017 by The Rosen Publishing Group, Inc.
29 East 21st Street, New York, NY 10010

Library of Congress Cataloging-in-Publication Data

Names: Lusted, Marcia Amidon, author.
Title: For people who love to repair things / Marcia Amidon Lusted.
Description: First edition. | New York : Rosen Publishing, [2017] | Series:
  Cool careers without college | Includes bibliographical references and
  index.
Identifiers: LCCN 2016018107 | ISBN 9781508172840 (library bound)
Subjects: LCSH: Repairing—Vocational guidance—Juvenile literature. |
  Engineering technicians—Vocational guidance—Juvenile literature.
Classification: LCC TA157 .L686 2017 | DDC 620/.0046023—dc23
LC record available at https://lccn.loc.gov/2016018107

Manufactured in Malaysia

CONTENTS

INTRODUCTION

According to the news, or the warnings of guidance counselors, it can seem like finding a good job today is impossible without a college degree or other kinds of training. But some students are already good at fixing things. When something breaks, their family and friends call them. People like this like figuring out mechanical problems as if they're giant puzzles or enjoy finding a way to make something work better with just a little tweaking. Maybe they are fascinated with systems like plumbing and electricity or new technologies that are just beginning to get attention, like solar energy. If a student doesn't want to spend the kind of money that an advanced education costs, or attending college just isn't something they're ready to do right now, can they get a job with these skills and a high school diploma?

For someone who likes to fix things, there are many job possibilities, including fixing engines that are as large as those on a cruise ship or as small as this motorcycle engine.

The good news is that yes, people with an ability to fix things can get a good job based on those natural interests and aptitudes. If they are good at repairing items or systems, then there are even more options. Some jobs are available with a high school diploma, and perhaps with some vocational technical classes at the high school level, while some require an apprentice program, on-the-job training, and perhaps a certificate from a training program. For example, for people with a talent for tinkering with engines, there are many different types of mechanic jobs. If they're good with electrical stuff, there are plenty of job options in computer, electrician, and energy industries. If they really like working with their hands to make something, not just fix it, then there are construction jobs. Many of these jobs desperately need good people to fill them, and employers will hire people at an entry level and then help them get the training they need. Some have detailed programs for moving from apprentice to a master level, where trained workers can start their own company. And if people are intrigued by the idea of traveling the world, they can also get the training for many of these kinds of jobs while enlisted in the military. It will also provide a lifetime's worth of job skills.

Each chapter in this book will explore one kind of job that a skilled fix-it person can start working in, right out of high school. It describes what kinds of classes can be taken while still in high school to prepare for the job, as well as the aptitudes that make someone a good fit for this kind of job. Some jobs require more training than others, and many have options for advancement if you do decide to take some college-level courses. Each chapter describes the job, what a typical day is like, and what to expect as to training and job outlook. Each job description also has places to go for more information.

CHAPTER 1

CRUISE SHIP MECHANIC

It might not seem like it's even a job, sailing all over the world on a cruise ship, enjoying sunshine and blue skies and the ocean waves. But working as a cruise ship mechanic isn't just fun, games, and getting a tan. It's an important job, and the health and safety of the crew and passengers depend on it.

A cruise ship mechanic is also referred to as an engineer, although this does not mean that the mechanic has an engineering degree. Their primary responsibility is the maintenance and repair of the ship's engines, as well as pumps, generators, and the other machinery needed to run the ship and its systems. There is always a mechanic on duty in the engine room, so they work in rotating shifts to make sure that the engines are always running smoothly, day and night.

The team of cruise ship mechanics monitors the engines, boilers, pumps, generators, and electrical equipment. They run diagnostics on equipment to identify any problems and

The engines on a cruise ship are large and complex and require constant maintenance of both moving parts and other systems. Often mechanics work specific shifts on a team, as maintenance is on a twenty-four-hour cycle.

make sure that everything is functioning properly. They do maintenance (except for large overhauls or problems that require the ship to be in a port) and replace any components that are faulty or old. They must be good at diagnosing and fixing common problems, since these problems might arise when the ship is far out to sea or far from a maintenance facility.

Cruise ship mechanics must also be willing to spend long amounts of time away from home. Almost all mechanics must live onboard a ship, and they are hired for tours that last between six and eight months. It can be difficult for mechanics with families, since job stability comes only from frequent absences from home. But they are able to visit foreign countries and meet new people almost weekly.

A DAY IN THE LIFE OF A CRUISE SHIP MECHANIC

In the course of a regular day, a cruise ship mechanic is on rotating shifts of regular watch-keeping. The mechanic is familiar with line diagrams of all the pipelines in the engine room, including fuel lines and bilge (wastewater) lines. He also knows the location of all the emergency exits, fire extinguishers, and blowers in the room. During his or her eight-hour shift, either in a morning, afternoon,

Mechanics must be familiar with every part of the systems that run huge ship engines, including electrical, piping, and wastewater. These are critical for the safety and comfort of the passengers and crew.

or overnight slot, the mechanic will be performing many tasks, including:

- Perform the start-up procedure for all the machinery, such as the diesel generators, pumps, boilers, and, of course, the main engines

The engines of a large ship require the constant monitoring of gauges to make sure that everything is running properly and safely. The engine requires constant observation and maintenance.

- Dismantle, diagnose, repair, and reassemble broken parts of many systems
- Ensure that stand-by equipment is in good working order
- Cover emergency situations, even if off duty, and work throughout the emergency until it is resolved
- Monitor activity taking place in the engine room during his or her shift, such as gauge readings and the results of any testing of equipment
- Track inventory of new, spare, and repair parts

A mechanic is also expected to keep logs of some of the activity taking place in the engine room during his or her shift, such as gauge readings and the results of any testing of equipment. They may also need to keep an inventory of spare and repair parts and request new parts when they are needed.

An engine room is hot and humid, as well as extremely noisy. The mechanic is constantly surrounded by potentially dangerous machinery. Working on the ship's systems may require being in uncomfortable or cramped areas, as well as in stressful situations. Being able to communicate and work as a team is extremely important.

PREPARING YOURSELF

The key skill needed to find work as a cruise ship mechanic is mechanical aptitude. Besides experience working with engines and other mechanical systems, it is helpful to take any vocational training classes in mechanical systems and engines that might be offered in high school. A ship mechanic does need to obtain a special license, the Transportation Worker Identification Credential (TWIC).

As a federal US Coast Guard requirement, those seeking to earn the TWIC card must first go through extensive background checks to verify their identity and any potential wrongdoings. To make the process as smooth as possible, applicants should compile the following:

LIFE AT SEA

Like all personnel on board a cruise ship when the weather becomes bad, mechanics have to not only cope with bad weather, but to continue to work through it, even if they feel seasick or conditions are dangerous. In fact, they may be needed even more during a storm if it affects the ship's systems. Storms are a fact of life on the ocean, but most cruise ships will adjust their itinerary so that they can avoid any large and potentially hazardous storms. Cruise ships, unlike cargo ships, are dedicated to giving their passengers a good experience. Cargo ships have tight schedules to keep and are less likely to go out of their way or into a port just to avoid a storm. Cruise ships have three options during a severe storm such as a hurricane: find a safe port, alter their course to avoid the storm, or at least stay out of sea where there is less chance of running into anything and damaging the ship.

- Proof of citizenship
- Maritime training documentation
- Proof of sea experience
- Successful passing of drug and medical examinations
- Character references

While many mechanic positions do not require a certificate or special training program, many modern ships now use a combination of diesel, gas, and electrical technologies for propulsion and systems, as well as computer technology. They need mechanics who are able to work with all of these systems. Many community colleges and vocational training schools offer programs in diesel mechanics and other systems, and some shipping companies may require some sort of certificate from a program like this. Some programs in diesel and marine engineering include hands-on experience as well as periods of time at sea. Another way to access the training for a mechanic job is to enlist in the US Navy and gain skills and training there which can be used for a cruise ship job after the enlistment period is over.

FUTURE PROSPECTS

Employment for marine engineers, which is the category that a cruise ship mechanic falls under, is expected to grow at a rate of about 9 percent, better than the average for most occupations. The entire industry of water transportation is expected to continue growing, not only for transportation of goods, but also for pleasure. According to the US Department of Labor, cruise ship mechanics are in demand; the level of training that a mechanic is willing to achieve will help them find more job opportunities.

FOR MORE INFORMATION

BOOKS

Calder, Nigel. *Marine Diesel Engines: Maintenance, Troubleshooting, and Repair*. 3rd ed. Camden, ME: Ragged Mountain Press, 2006.
Calder is considered to be the world's best expert on diesel engines after working as a diesel mechanic for thirty-five years. This book is a small scale beginner's guide to diesel engines used on boats, intended for do-it-yourself boat owners.

Rauf, Don, and Monique Vescia. *Choose Your Own Career Adventure on a Cruise Ship*. North Mankato, MN: Cherry Lake Publishing, 2016.
Intended for young readers, this book presents eight different scenarios and experiences for a taste of what it's like to work at some of the jobs that are available on cruise ships.

McDavid, Richard A., and Susan Echaore-McDavid. *Career Opportunities in Transportation*. New York, NY: Ferguson Publishing, 2009.
This book explains both familiar and not-so-familiar careers in the transportation industry, with profiles of jobs like chartering sightseeing boats, working as a deckhand, and being a federal air marshall.

Ross, David. *Visual Encyclopedia of Ships*. Minneapolis, MN: Chartwell Books, 2013.
This is a good visual identification guide to every type of ship, past and present, from Viking longships to today's military ships. The author is a professional historian who specializes in transportation topics.

ORGANIZATIONS

Association of Diesel Specialists
400 Admiral Boulevard
Kansas City, MO 64106
(816) 285-0810
Website: http://diesel.org
This organization is the worldwide trade association of the diesel industry and helps its members to achieve success through its programs and services.

Cruise Line International Association (CLIA)
1201 F Street NW, Suite 250
Washington, DC 20004
(202) 759-9370
Website: http://www.cruising.org

This is the worldwide trade association for the cruise industry and related partners in the travel industry. It educates and works on behalf of its members.

PERIODICALS

Marine Reporter and Engineering News
118 E. 25th Street, 2nd Floor
New York, NY 10010-2977
(212) 477-6700
Website: http://magazines.marinelink.com/Magazines/
MaritimeReporter/201512
This publication is for the worldwide professional shipping and maritime industry, including ships and ship technology. This publisher releases a variety of magazines that are all related to shipping, marine technology, and offshore energy industries.

BLOGS

Marine Engineering: A Voyage to Become a
Chief Engineer...
Website: http://shreyasnaik.blogspot.com

This blog, published by a company that supplies parts and equipment for ships and related industries, covers marine engineering and related topics. Posts include discussion of more "green" shipping technologies, arctic drilling, and environmental concerns around offshore oil drilling.

World Wide Metric blog
Website: http://blog.worldwidemetric.com/blog
Shreyas Naik, who is an engineer for the Shipping Corporation of India, writes this blog about the process of becoming a chief engineer on a commercial ship, what it's actually like working on a ship, and other related topics.

WEBSITES

Due to the changing nature of internet links, Rosen Publishing has developed an online list of websites related to the subject of this book. This site is updated regularly. Please use this link to access the list:

http://www.rosenlinks.com/CCWC/repair

CHAPTER 2

PIPE FITTER/STEAMFITTER

Most people think that plumbers, steamfitters, and pipe fitters are all the same thing. It's true that all three professions deal with assembling and fitting pipes. But most plumbers work on the residential level, putting plumbing into new homes or repairing existing plumbing. Pipe fitters and steamfitters, on the other hand, are more likely to work on industrial buildings, like hospitals, commercial buildings, factories, and apartment buildings. They might be self-employed, but they also work for companies that construct large pipelines, for plants that generate steam or nuclear power, utility companies, oil refineries, paper mills, auto factories, and gas and chemical plants.

What is the difference between a pipe fitter and a steamfitter? They work with the same basic materials and are both responsible for everything related to installing and maintaining pipe systems. They plan the layout for piping, make the sections they need from steel and other materials, assemble

Pipe fitters and steamfitters both perform maintenance and repair on piping systems. This can mean working on high- or low-pressure pipe systems.

the pipes and install them, and then maintain and repair the systems after they are completed and operating. They may also install sprinkler systems for fire prevention, which carry water, foam, carbon dioxide, or dry chemicals to put out fires. Both jobs also include installing and maintaining automatic controls and gauges. The difference is that pipe fitters work with both low pressure and high pressure systems. These systems are used in heating and cooling as well as in factories and for generating electricity. Steamfitters specialize in piping systems that are under very high pressure, such as steam, liquids, or gases. Their work can be more dangerous because of the potential for injury from high-pressure pipes and their contents.

The work done by steamfitters and pipe fitters includes installing all the pieces of a piping system, including valves, supports, and controls for the pipes. They need to be good at selecting the proper pipes and measuring and cutting them to size. It might be necessary to thread the pipes so that they can be attached to other pipes. They may need to cut openings in walls and floors and weld pipes, as well as read blueprints and interpret them to estimate costs and create a plan for a piping system. Installing sprinkler systems also includes installing sprinkler heads throughout a building, connecting the system to supply tanks or water mains, reading and interpreting specifications and fire codes, and testing the system for leaks. Every type of installation also requires future troubleshooting, maintenance, repair, and replacing of pipes that are leaking.

A DAY IN THE LIFE OF A STEAMFITTER OR PIPE FITTER

A typical day can vary widely, because steamfitters and pipe fitters work in so many different situations. If a company or an institution, such as a hospital or college, employs fitters, they spend all their time in that location, maintaining piping systems or working on whatever projects their company is doing at the moment. These jobs are usually regular forty-hour-a-week jobs, although more hours may be added during peak construction seasons. However, some pipe fitters and steamfitters prefer to travel from job to job, all over the country. They might spend months on the construction of a nuclear power plant's piping systems, then move on to a job on an offshore drilling rig. They may have to work outdoors and even live at a company camp or temporary housing. Many people in these professions like the variety of moving from job to job, both across the country and even overseas. No matter what the location or the job, however, steamfitters and pipe fitters will always be doing certain basic tasks:
- Cut, thread, and hammer pipe to specifications
- Assemble and secure pipes, tubes, and fittings

Pipe fitters can work in a variety of settings, from existing buildings to new construction, and in places like ships and oil drilling platforms.

- Cut and bore holes in walls and structures
- Attach pipes to walls, structures, and fixtures
- Inspect, diagnose, and test installed piping systems
- Measure and mark pipes for cutting and fitting
- Plan and draw new piping systems according to blueprints
- Select and order pipes and related materials

PREPARING YOURSELF

Steamfitting and pipe fitting are careers that do not require a college degree, although a high school diploma is necessary. It also helps to take any vocational training classes that are offered in high school. However, these jobs don't require any special technical certification for getting started, although it is possible to attend a training school. They do, however, work on the apprenticeship system.

An apprentice is someone who works and receives pay while being trained on how to do his or her job. They work alongside a journeyman steamfitter, with advanced knowledge and experience, which supervises their work and teaches them. An apprenticeship lasts four to five years and combines on-the-job training with classroom time, which is offered by businesses and labor unions and is usually paid for by the employer or by the state where the apprentice is working. During each year of their apprenticeship, the apprentice must have 1,700 to 2,000 hours of job experience and a minimum of 246 hours of technical education. This includes classroom learning about safety, the local plumbing codes and regulations, and how to read blueprints. It can also include mathematics, physics, and chemistry. To become an apprentice, students must be eighteen and high school graduates, pass a drug screening and a basic math test, and be

Like many construction trades, pipe fitters usually learn on the job, as apprentices to experienced pipe fitters. The role between an apprentice and an expert is called a journeyman.

WOMEN, TOO

Steamfitting and pipe fitting may seem like jobs that are done mostly by men. But there are plenty of women who enjoy this work just as much. Susan Miller has worked as a pipe fitter for more than twenty-seven years. Interviewed by TheGrindstone.com in 2012, she explains she enjoys the travel and moving around. "Sometimes the jobs only last a couple of months, and sometimes they last a year. You just work until you've built the unit and you're on to the next one…I usually try to find jobs where I'm just working 9 months and go home in the summer." Even though she has found that she hasn't advanced as far in her career as men do, she still feels it's a good career for women. "It's hard work, but it's a gratifying career with a very good paycheck. A lot of women make good welders." Miller plans to work as a pipe fitter until she retires. "I will probably do this until I retire because I love it. I love to build a power plant or a solar field, and drive by it and say, 'I helped build that.'"

computer literate. After they complete their apprenticeship, they become journeyman pipe fitters and steamfitters and can get jobs anywhere. They can also continue their education and become master-level fitters, which is often required to start their own business.

FUTURE PROSPECTS

As with many occupations that involve trades like plumbing, electricity, and heating, the demand for qualified workers is growing. According to the Bureau of Labor Statistics, the field is expected to grow about 12 percent, which is higher than the average for other occupations. The construction and retrofitting of power plants and factories may increase demand for pipe fitters and steamfitters, and some employers have difficulty finding qualified workers. As the Baby Boomer generation ages, many plumbers, pipe fitters, and steamfitters are expected to retire as well. For people who like to work with their hands, analyze systems, and do careful, precise work, it's a great field to be entering right now.

FOR MORE INFORMATION

BOOKS

Gregory, Josh. *21st Century Skills Library: Cool Careers Plumber*. North Makato, MN: Cherry Lake, 2011.
Written for young readers, this book discusses the different skills involved in being a plumber, as well as the training and experience needed to do the job.

Hart, C. L. *Pipe Layout Helps: For the Pipefitter and Welder*. 6th ed. Clinton, NC: Construction Trades Press, 2006.
This book is a practical construction guide to how to create layouts for piping in plumbing and pipe fitting work, written by a professional pipe fitter.

Lindsey, Forrest R. *Pipefitters Handbook: Second Expanded Edition*. Eastford, CT: Martino Fine Books, 2012.
This book, which provides practical information about bending, laying out, and installing pipes and other plumbing work, was written based on the author's thirty-five years of experience as a pipe fitter.

PHCC Educational Foundation, *Plumbing 101*, 6th ed. Boston, MA: Cengage Learning, 2012.

This book is produced by the Plumbing-Heating-
Cooling Contractors (PHCC) Educational
Foundation and provides simple, straightforward
explanations of real-world plumbing situations
and problems.

ORGANIZATIONS

United Association Union of Plumbers, Fitters,
Welders & Service Techs
Three Park Place
Annapolis, MD 21401
(410) 269-2000
Website: http://www.ua.org
This labor union represents 340,000 members of the
plumbers and fitters industry in the United States
and Canada. It provides training and certification for
new plumbers and pipe fitters, and helps existing
plumbing contractors grow their businesses.

PERIODICALS

Constructor
5950 NW First Place
Gainesville, FL 32607

(800) 369-6220

Website: http://www.constructormagazine.com

This magazine offers in-depth coverage and analysis of the construction industry and related topics, such as insurance, safety, and regulatory issues, as well as practical advice on labor relations and legal matters.

WEBSITES

Due to the changing nature of internet links, Rosen Publishing has developed an online list of websites related to the subject of this book. This site is updated regularly. Please use this link to access the list:

http://www.rosenlinks.com/CCWC/repair

CHAPTER 3

AVIATION MECHANIC

Whether you're watching an airshow from the ground or taking a flight across the country, there is something fascinating about airplanes. Many people like to be around them but don't necessarily want to fly them. Or perhaps they're interested in flying, but also want to know how airplanes work and how to keep them running smoothly and safely. For these kinds of people, working as an aviation mechanic might be the perfect career.

An aviation, or aircraft, mechanic is basically the person who carries out the repair and maintenance of the mechanical or avionics equipment that makes airplanes and helicopters fly safely. The aviation mechanic inspects the aircraft and its systems, makes necessary repairs, and makes sure that the electronic, structural, and mechanical elements of an aircraft are all in good working order. They keep an eye on the parts of the aircraft and repair or replace anything that's worn out. They know how to use various tools and diagnostic devices, as well as computers and manuals, to keep the aircraft maintained to the standards that are set by the Federal Aviation Administration (FAA).

Being an aviation mechanic requires some skills that are common to people who like to fix things. They need to have manual dexterity, because they will spend a lot of time pulling things apart and putting them back together. They need to be detail-oriented so that they can meet very exact standards. The technical skill to be able to read instruments and gauges as well as other diagnostic tools is also important. And they must be good at troubleshooting so that they can discover the cause of a problem and then fix it.

There are specializations within the category of aviation mechanic. General mechanics are the ones who complete a basic aircraft mechanics class and get a certificate. For those looking to upgrade their skills or who wish to have more specialization, there are other categories. Avionics technicians focus on the electronic systems that airplanes use for things like altitude, weather, radio communications, and autopilot systems. Avionics mechanics can also train in other aspects of airplane maintenance and are one of the most versatile categories of mechanics. Airframe mechanics are trained to work on all of the structural elements of an aircraft, excluding the engines, propellers, and avionic instruments. Power plant mechanics work on the engines or power plants of an aircraft. A and P mechanics are a

Aircraft mechanics often work on maintaining and repairing huge aircraft engines, like this one from a Boeing 737 jet.

combination of airframe and power plant mechanics and are qualified to do both jobs.

A DAY IN THE LIFE OF AN AVIATION MECHANIC

Depending on what kind they are, aviation mechanics can work in different conditions and locations. They might work inside a hangar, on the flight line (the area around hangars where planes are loaded, unloaded, and serviced), or in repair shops. They may be working in inclement or harsh weather conditions and at any time of the day or night. Some of these tasks may be:

- Diagnose mechanical or electrical problems
- Test aircraft parts with gauges and other diagnostic equipment
- Keep records of maintenance and repair work
- Repair wings, brakes, electrical systems, and other aircraft components
- Replace defective parts using hand tools or power tools

Working on a jet engine often means working within the aircraft itself, surrounded by wires and cables. Most technicians can be found in airport or private airfields, but there are also positions in other commercial roles.

Aircraft mechanics must learn how to work on many different types of aircraft, from small propeller airplanes to huge jets.

PREPARING YOURSELF

It is not absolutely required to have a high school diploma in order to start training as an aviation mechanic, but since most employers prefer it, it makes sense to have one. High school classes in math, physics, computer science, chemistry, and

WHAT'S WHAT

An airplane is a complex system that needs a lot of attention and maintenance. Here are key parts of an airplane that mechanics focus on:

- Wings provide lift to keep the plane aloft and store fuel.
- Flaps help slow down the plane, because airplanes don't have brakes.
- De-icing systems remove ice from aircraft that's too big for a window scraper.
- The power plant/engine, along with the fuel pressure and pumps and delivery system, directs the fuel and cooling systems to keep temperatures steady.
- The rudder/aileron helps steer and control the movement of the plane.
- Landing gear cushions the plane and allows it to land and move on the ground.
- The propeller is a huge eggbeater that drives the airplane through the sky.
- Avionics systems are navigational internal electronics controls and monitoring systems, as well as radio/communication systems that direct the plane.

English are a good background because an aviation mechanic needs to be able to understand the physical principles involved in actually getting an airplane to fly. Some high schools have avionics programs or partnerships with aviation schools, and those courses can be extremely helpful.

While some beginning aviation mechanics get their training on the job, others take an FAA-approved Aviation Mechanics Technician course. Completing the course allows the student to receive a certificate recognized by the FAA. Without the course, on-the-job training must include eighteen months of practical experience with either power plants or airframes or thirty months of experience on both. Whether trained on the job or with a course certificate, all mechanics must pass an FAA exam that consists of a written test, an oral exam, and a practical test. Once they pass this, they can be licensed as airframe, power plant, or A and P mechanics. The exception is avionics technicians, who usually have an associate's degree because of the increasing complexity of avionics systems.

FUTURE PROSPECTS

Aircraft and avionics mechanics jobs are not expected to change much in the near future. According to the Bureau of Labor Statistics, while air traffic may increase, newer aircraft are expected to require less maintenance than older models. Outsourced, specialized roles are considered the most efficient way to handle airline maintenance, which limits the growth of the number of technicians working in the field. The best opportunities for continued employment will be with mechanics who have degrees or certificates for all different aspects of airplane maintenance and repair.

FOR MORE INFORMATION

BOOKS

Crane, Dale. *Aviation Mechanic Handbook: The Aviation Standard*. 6th ed. Newcastle, WA: Aviation Supplies and Academics, 2012.

The author, an airframe and power plant aviation mechanic, wrote this guide as a pocket-sized reference with many of the standards and information needed by aviation mechanics on a regular basis for maintaining and servicing aircraft.

Gregory, Josh. *Cool Military Careers: Avionics Technician*. North Mankato, MN: Cherry Lake Publishing, 2013.

Written as part of a series on military careers, this book is a guide to how some aviation mechanics are trained while enlisted in the military, including job requirements and how military aircraft techs can find jobs in the civilian world after their service.

Rhatigan, Joe. *Get a Job at the Airport*. North Mankato, MN: Cherry Lake Publishing, 2016.

Written from the point of view of a fictional airport worker, this book explores all the different jobs that can be done at an airport. It also includes writing prompts and activities.

ORGANIZATIONS

Aircraft Mechanics Fraternal Association (AMFA)
14001 E Iliff Avenue, Suite 217
Aurora, CO 80014
(303) 752-AMFA (2632)
Website: http://www.amfanational.org
This union represents aircraft maintenance technicians
and people in related jobs. It protects the rights
and privileges of its members and works to raise
the standards of and increase recognition of the
profession of aircraft mechanics.

Association for Women in Aviation Maintenance
(AWAM)
2330 Kenlee Drive
Cincinnati, OH 45230
(386) 416-0248
Website: http://www.awam.org
AWAM is a nonprofit organization formed for the
purpose of supporting women's professional growth
and enrichment in the aviation maintenance fields.

Professional Aviation Maintenance Association
(PAMA)
400 North Washington Street, Suite 300
Alexandria, VA 22314

(877) 901-5410
Website: http://pama.wildapricot.org
This association for aviation maintenance technicians
provides education, communication, and support.

PERIODICALS

AirMaintenance Update
7–11771 Horseshoe Way
Richmond, BC V7A 4V4
Canada
(604) 214-9824
Website: http://amumagazine.com
This publication is a Canadian magazine specifically
for air maintenance professionals. It includes
technical and job-related articles, as well as job
listings and links for more information.

BLOGS

Aircraft Maintenance and Tools blog
Website: http://aircraftmaintenanceandtools.blogspot
.com
This is a professional blog by an aviation mechanic
about what it's really like to work in the field,
including working in an airport, regulations, and
hands-on information.

Aviation Institute of Maintenance blog
Website: http://www.aviationmaintenance.edu/blog
Published by the Aviation Institute of Maintenance,
this blog is about what it's really like to work as an
aviation mechanic. It also has interesting industry
news and career training information.

VIDEO

YouTube: "Aircraft Maintenance Engineer"
Website: https://www.youtube.com/
watch?v=bNvwz8r_300&nohtml5=False
In this video, an aircraft mechanic shows some of the
basic tasks and responsibilities involved in her job, as
well as the skills and training needed.

YouTube: "What is an Aircraft Mechanic?"
Website: https://www.youtube.com/
watch?v=ELUC5C74Mpc
This video invites viewers to try the career of an
aircraft mechanic for five minutes. It shows some
of the skills and activities involved and talks about
required training and licensing.

WEBSITES

Due to the changing nature of internet links, Rosen Publishing has developed an online list of websites related to the subject of this book. This site is updated regularly. Please use this link to access the list:

http://www.rosenlinks.com/CCWC/repair

CHAPTER 4

HVAC TECHNICIAN

Most people don't give much thought to all the systems in their houses until something goes wrong with them and help is needed. Plumbers and electricians are pretty straightforward, but who do you call when your heating or air-conditioning needs to be fixed? A heating/ ventilation/air-conditioning/refrigeration (HVAC or HVACR) technician is the one who fixes these systems in homes and buildings. Specifically, they deal with heating, air-conditioning, and refrigeration systems, both installing them and repairing them. They regulate temperature, humidity, and air quality in buildings, depending on the climate, to create a climate-controlled interior environment. They may also work on the refrigeration systems that keep food and medicine from spoiling during storage or transportation. HVAC technicians usually focus on either installation or repair. Some specialize even further in areas such as solar energy, radiant heating, commercial refrigeration, or testing.

HVAC technicians may spend a large amount of time working outside on equipment such as this rooftop air-conditioning unit. HVAC maintenance can be a physically demanding profession.

HVAC technician may work repairing and maintaining complex heating and cooling systems for large buildings.

HVAC technicians need to have good mechanical skills, since much of their job requires taking things apart, fixing them, and putting them back together. Good customer service and people skills are also important, as well as good time management, especially if the tech needs to be on call and juggling appointments at homes and businesses. It is also vital to be able to troubleshoot problems with systems and what might be causing them, as well as how to fix them.

These systems are made up of many different parts, including electrical, mechanical, and electronic parts like thermostats, fans, ducts, motors, and pipes. Workers must have the ability to provide maintenance and identify problems and carry out repairs on any part of the system. Technicians carry out this work by making adjustments to the system settings and running performance tests of the system.

HVAC technicians work in many different types of places. They may work for a company, within a large facility as a resident technician, or be self-employed. They work mostly in homes, schools, stores, hospitals, office buildings, or factories and might make service calls or be assigned to a single job site for an entire day. While most work is done inside, there may be times when the tech has to work outside on heat exchanger equipment. Even inside, they might have to work in cramped spaces or in buildings where there's no heating or cooling because the system is broken. HVAC techs do have one of the highest rates of illness and injury among all occupations. They can suffer from electrical shock and burns, as well as muscle fatigue and injuries from lifting heavy equipment.

A DAY IN THE LIFE OF AN HVAC TECHNICIAN

For an HVAC technician, no two days are alike, especially if they are on call and traveling to different locations with

HVAC technicians who work in potentially dangerous environments, such as rooftops, often wear safety equipment to prevent falls while they carry out inspections and repairs.

different problems to solve or installations to do. But there are some tasks that are basic to most HVAC work:

- Use blueprints or design specifications to install or repair HVACR systems
- Connect systems to fuel and water supply lines, air ducts, and other components

- Install electrical wiring and controls and test for their proper operation
- Inspect and maintain customers' HVACR systems
- Test individual components to determine and make necessary repairs
- Determine HVACR systems' energy use and make recommendations to improve their efficiency

An HVAC tech also uses a variety of tools, from the basics like hammers, metal snips, pipe benders, and cutters and drills, to more specific tools like gauges for measuring and acetylene torches for working on refrigerant lines and air ducts. Testing tools are important, such as thermometers and pressure gauges, as well as voltmeters to test electrical current and monometers to test pressure. Work with chemical refrigerants requires a special exam and licensing by the Environmental Protection Agency (EPA), because they are an environmental hazard.

PREPARING YOURSELF

Like many trades that have to do with building systems, most HVAC technicians receive their training through the apprentice system. This means that they are hired by an HVAC contractor or company and receive pay while they are trained on the job. To become an apprentice, a student must have graduated from high school, and it's helpful to have taken any related vocational training classes that the

THE SMART HOUSE

One of the growing home technologies that affect HVAC systems is the idea of a "smart house." Like factories and commercial buildings before them, smart houses are automated so that the house is always comfortable and secure. Smart house technology can also be controlled from a computer or smart phone, allowing home owners to adjust the temperature, turn on the lights, and control entry and surveillance. For HVAC in particular, this means new thermostats that control heating and cooling, special vents that can control the temperature in every room, window air conditioners that "talk" to the home's master computer, and energy-efficient lightbulbs that turn on and off automatically through a computerized hub.

school offers. Math and physics classes, as well as a basic understanding of plumbing and electricity, are also a good foundation for an HVAC apprentice program. An apprenticeship generally lasts three to five years and is a combination of 2,000 hours of on-the-job experience and 144 hours of classroom training. Apprentices learn safety practices, how to read blueprints, and the functions of HVAC systems. Some states require HVAC techs to be licensed and that means passing a state exam at the end of the apprenticeship. It is also possible to take further training and exams to become ed in more specialized areas such as working on oil-burning furnaces or with compressed-air refrigeration systems. Some HVAC techs also earn two-year certificates or degrees from colleges or vocational training schools.

FUTURE PROSPECTS

It's a good time to become an HVAC technician. HVAC jobs are expected to grow by 14 percent in the coming years, much faster than the average for all occupations. This is because of the growth in construction of new homes and buildings, as well as the increase in sophisticated climate control systems. With more emphasis on environmentally friendly and energy efficient systems, more HVAC techs will be needed to install new systems or update existing ones. And because the systems in buildings and homes are constantly in need of repair and replacement, HVACs will always be needed for those jobs as well. Techs who are willing to get advanced training, especially in computers and electronics, will also find themselves in demand for newer, more complex systems of heating and cooling.

FOR MORE INFORMATION

BOOKS

Bickerstaff, Linda. *Careers in Heating, Ventilation, and Air-Conditioning (HVAC)*. New York, NY: Rosen, 2013.
This book provides young readers with an overview of the many different kinds of careers in the HVAC field, including the necessary training.

Meyer, Leo A. *Careers in the HVAC Industry*. Hayward, CA: LAMA Books, 2004.
Part of the Indoor Environmental Technician's Library, this title is an overview of the field, from a publishing company that specializes in HVAC information.

Silberstein, Eugene. *Residential Construction Academy HVAC*. 2nd ed. Farmington Hills, MI: Cengage Learning, 2011.
Written by an HVAS field technician and systems designer, this book covers training materials with practical information based on the National Association of Home Builders.

ORGANIZATIONS

Air Conditioning Contractors of America
2800 Shirlington Road #300
Arlington, VA 22206
888-290-2220
Website: http://www.acca.org
This association is for people who work in the indoor
    environment and energy services community and
    provides communication, marketing, and education.

American Society of Heating, Refrigerating and
Air-Conditioning Engineers
ASHRAE Headquarters
1791 Tullie Circle, NE
Atlanta, GA 30329
(404) 636-8400
Website: https://www.ashrae.org
This is a global society advancing human well-being
    through sustainable technology for the built
    environment, focusing on building systems,
    energy efficiency, indoor air quality, refrigeration,
    and sustainability.

PERIODICALS

ACHR News
2401 W. Big Beaver Road, Suite 700
Troy, MI 48084
(248) 362-3700
Website: http://www.achrnews.com
The *ACHR News* has practical articles on new
technologies, troubleshooting and repairs, business
and financing advice, and educational information for
HVAC technicians and business owners.

HVACR Business
24651 Center Ridge Road, Suite 425
Westlake, OH 44145
(440) 471-7810
Website: http://hvacrbusiness.com
This magazine focuses on the business of running a
HVACR company, including articles on training and
education, staffing, financing, and legal issues.

WEBSITES

Due to the changing nature of internet links, Rosen Publishing has developed an online list
of websites related to the subject of this book. This site is updated regularly. Please use this link to access the list:

http://www.rosenlinks.com/CCWC/repair

CHAPTER 5

SOLAR PANEL TECHNICIAN

More and more, people are searching for green, renewable ways to generate energy for homes, businesses, and even cars. One of these green technologies is solar power, which uses photovoltaic cells to capture the energy of the sun and generate electricity. Solar panels on the roofs of homes and businesses, as well as powering streetlights and street signs, are becoming more common. As solar panels proliferate, there is an increasing need for people who know how to install and repair them properly. These people are called solar photovoltaic (PV) installers or, more commonly, solar panel installers.

The scope of an installer's work depends on whether he or she works independently or the size of the company that employs him or her. Generally, solar panel installers are responsible for designing a solar system that fits the location

Solar energy technicians perform work such as installing solar modules on rooftops. Many modules are installed and linked as a solar panel to provide electricity.

Installing a solar energy system on a building involves design, planning, installation, and electrical systems, requiring people in different roles working together as a team.

and the structure. Then they have to measure, trim, and attach the solar modules to a framework and attach the solar panels to the roof of a structure. The panels are heavy and fragile and must be handled carefully. The installer has to make sure the panels fit securely and are aligned in the correct direction for maximum solar exposure. The panels must also be sealed against weather. Once they are in place, the installer must then make the electrical connections needed to bring the power into the building, either directly to the electrical panel or to storage batteries. The system must meet the building codes and safety codes for the area and be tested. For this reason, many solar installers are also electricians, and some states require the installers to be licensed. Installers may also be troubleshooting and repairing problems with existing panels and connections.

An installer may be an independent contractor or may work for a larger company. Installers are often just on the first rung of the solar industry. With advanced training, they can work their way up to becoming a solar contractor with a business of their own, a solar instructor, or a project manager. They might become solar designers, who decide how best to use solar technology on new and existing buildings. Solar installers can also get their plumbing or electrician licenses and expand their knowledge and skills in those areas as well.

A DAY IN THE LIFE OF A SOLAR PANEL INSTALLER

The tasks that an installer does in a typical day will depend on whether they work independently or as part of a team. But generally, they will be doing task such as:

- Plan PV system design based on customer needs, expectations, and site conditions
- Install solar modules, panels, or support structures in accordance with building codes and standards

- Connecting PV panels to the power grid and testing equipment
- Applying weather sealing to equipment being installed
- Perform routine PV system maintenance

Because they work as much outside as inside, installers must deal with harsh weather conditions, and they must be able to deal with heights, since much of the outside work is done on rooftops. An installer also needs to be strong and able to lift panels that might weigh forty or fifty pounds (eighteen or twenty-two kilograms), as well as having mechanical and construction skills.

PREPARING YOURSELF

There are a few different paths to becoming a solar panel installer, but no matter what, a high school diploma is required. High school vocational classes in construction, wiring, plumbing, math, and physics are helpful. Many installers start out as electricians or plumbers and will go through apprentice programs and licensing for those careers and then train to be solar installers. Solar panel installers learn their job either through direct on-the-job training by an employer, by attending a certificate or degree program at a community college or vocation training school, or through training by a solar equipment manufacturer. Organizations like Solar Energy International also offer training programs

UP ON THE ROOF

Jason Edens, a solar panel installer, says there is no typical day at work for him. In his interview with MnEnergyCareers in 2016, he notes that every day is unique. For Edens, whose company handles both manufacturing and installation, the work varies across projects. "As an organization, we do a lot of solar heating and solar electric. There's a lot of prep in doing and managing the solar energy installations," he notes. As an integrated manufacturer and installer, his company has a lot of different people doing different things. It's a combination of deskwork and fieldwork. He explains, "There's a lot of engineering time, time spent crunching numbers, time spent on the actual manufacturing and selling of our product. It takes a lot of pieces to put the puzzle together." Because of the variety of work involved in the solar industry, his advice is to get involved as soon as you can. "Get your hands dirty — volunteer, figure out if it's what you want to do and if it's a good match with your skill set.

in solar energy occupations. Solar energy installation is a job that has not yet been regulated by the government as to licensing and training, and the quality and length of training can vary widely. Many solar installers are licensed as general contractors and through the North American Board of Certified Energy Practitioners (NABCEP). Certification can improve the job prospects of installers, and many larger projects require workers to be certified.

Photovoltaic solar panels to create solar energy are becoming more popular all over the world, creating a growing industry for workers who are interested in solar careers.

FUTURE PROSPECTS

The US Department of Labor does not yet have statistics on the job outlook for solar installer jobs because it is a new occupation, but it is a field that is expected to continue growing at a rapid rate as more and more people turn to alternative energy sources and away from fossil fuels. Solar technicians are in short supply in many areas of the country, which means that new techs are needed. There are also an increasing number of companies installing solar panels because the cost of solar technology is coming down.

FOR MORE INFORMATION

BOOKS

Hantula, Richard. *Energy Today: Solar Power*. New York, NY: Chelsea House, 2010.
Written for young readers, this book discusses solar power, how it generates electricity, and how scientists are working on new and better ways to harness and develop solar energy.

Hantula, Richard. *How Do Solar Panels Work?* New York, NY: Chelsea House, 2009.
Part of the Science in the Real World series this book for young readers talks about the technology behind solar panels and how scientist are working to develop even better ways to use solar energy.

McNamee, Gregory. *Careers in Renewable Energy: Get a Green Energy Job*. 2nd ed. Masonville, CO: Pixyjack Press, 2014.
This book is a resource covering many different career areas within the renewable energy industries.

Otfinoski, Steven. *Calling All Innovators: A Career for You: Wind, Solar, and Geothermal Power*. New York, NY: Franklin Watts, 2015.
This book, intended for young readers, covers the history of alternative energy and the technologies

behind it, as well as the careers that are open in those fields.

Taylor-Butler, Christine. *Solar Energy*. North Mankato, MN: Cherry Lake Publishing, 2009.
Part of the Science Explorer series, this book shows young readers how to do experiments that help them learn about solar energy.

ORGANIZATIONS

American Solar Energy Society Office (ASES)
2525 Arapahoe Avenue, Suite E4-253
Boulder, CO 80302
(303) 443-3130
Website: http://www.ases.org
ASES is an association of solar professionals and supporters with the mission to inspire an era of energy innovation and speed the transition to a sustainable energy economy.

Solar Energy Industries Association (SEIA)
600 14th Street NW, Suite 400
Washington, DC 20005
(202) 682-0556
Website: http://www.seia.org

SEIA is a national trade association representing all organizations that promote, manufacture, install, and support the development of solar energy.

PERIODICALS

Solar Power World
Website: http://www.solarpowerworldonline.com
This online magazine for solar contractors, installers, and developers, proves news and information regarding solar installation, development, and technology and helps solar contractors grow their businesses.

Solar Today
American Solar Energy Society
2525 Arapahoe Avenue, Suite E4-253
Boulder, CO 80302
(303) 443–3130
Website: http://solartoday.org
Published by the American Solar Energy Society, *Solar Today* contains articles about solar technology and sustainable energy including news, new technologies, and case studies from the field.

BLOGS

Scientific American Solar at Home
Website: http://blogs.scientificamerican.com/solar-at-
home
This blog, sponsored by *Scientific American* magazine
and intended for homeowners who want to use solar
energy, has posts about solar technology and solar
energy in homes.

Solar Power World blog
Website: http://www.solarpowerworldonline.com/
category/solar-power-blog
This blog, sponsored by *Solar Power World* magazine,
includes posts about solar power innovations,
installation, and technology for both installers
and consumers.

APPS

Onyx Photovoltaic Estimation App
Website: http://www.onyxsolar.com/pv-apps.html
This free app lets you enter the value for the
photovoltaic installation area you have in mind,
select the photovoltaic technology, and display the
energy that would be generated and its equivalent
in avoided CO_2 emissions, hours of light, and electric
car mileage.

WEBSITES

Due to the changing nature of internet links, Rosen Publishing has developed an online list of websites related to the subject of this book. This site is updated regularly. Please use this link to access the list:

http://www.rosenlinks.com/CCWC/repair

CHAPTER 6

ELEVATOR TECHNICIAN

Elevators are complex machines, and their ability to function affects public safety. There's more to elevator maintenance than those inspection certificates that might be posted inside them. It takes a trained elevator technician to install, service, and repair elevators so that they are always safe to be ridden, whether they are installed in buildings with three stories or three hundred stories.

An elevator technician does not just work on elevators. They also install and service escalators, dumbwaiters (a small elevator to move goods between floors, not people), moving walkways, and chairlifts. Elevator technicians often specialize in installation, service, or repair, especially since maintenance and repair involve a wider knowledge of electronics, hydraulics, and electricity. Elevators and related equipment are also becoming more and more computerized. But elevators still run on things like cables, gears, and braking systems that require hands-on mechanic skills.

Repairing and maintaining elevators is an interesting and challenging job, making it a competitive field for workers.

Repairing an escalator has its own unique set of challenges, with tight spaces and complex systems of operation. Technicians will often be well versed in both elevator and escalator maintenance.

Once an elevator has been installed and then fine-tuned by an elevator adjuster, it will be inspected annually to grease and oil moving parts and replace anything that seems worn. Most elevator service techs will visit the same elevators over and over again, performing annual maintenance as well as being on call if there are any problems. Extreme repairs usually require an elevator service crew that is used for heavier work, such as replacing cables, doors, or machine bearings. These tasks usually require heavier tools as well, such as cutting torches and rigging equipment, which regular elevator service techs aren't likely to carry with them. These service crews also do major alterations and upgrades, such as replacing motors, hydraulic pumps, and control panels.

A DAY IN THE LIFE OF AN ELEVATOR TECHNICIAN

An average day for an elevator tech is going to be different depending on whether they specialize in installation, adjustment, service, or repair, but there are tasks that they typically do:

- Read blueprints to determine the equipment needed for installation or repair

- Install, adjust, or repair elevator doors, cables, motors, and control systems
- Locate malfunctions in brakes, motors, switches, and control systems
- Connect electrical wiring to control panels and electric motors
- Use test equipment, such as ammeters and voltmeters, to diagnose problems
- Comply with safety regulations and building codes
- Keep service records of all maintenance and repair tasks

Elevator techs might work in businesses, hospitals, malls, restaurants, and private homes, depending on the equipment. While some service and installation crews work in teams, troubleshooting and servicing techs often work alone. While techs usually work a forty-hour week, they may be on call during all or some of that time and might be called out to repair jobs at night or on weekends, especially in situations where people are trapped inside a malfunctioning elevator. Because of the nature of elevators, techs may find themselves having to work in small, cramped spaces and in uncomfortable positions. They must also handle heavy equipment and must be physically fit and strong. Wearing safety equipment such as goggles, hard hats, and safety harnesses is a standard part of the work as well.

LIKE A PUZZLE

Alex Zion, an elevator technician in Virginia Beach, Virginia, spoke about his job in the *Virginian-Pilot* in 2012, detailing the rewards and responsibilities of the work. For him, the most rewarding part is figuring out the puzzle of troubleshooting. Zion explains the process: "You break out the prints, you take some visuals, you look at some things. You work through it like a puzzle." One of the most important parts of the job is rescuing people trapped in the elevator, which can happen with a power failure or other technical issue. Safety is the main concern, though the issues are usually resolved quickly. "You get trapped calls maybe once or twice a month, at most. Someone is literally stuck in an elevator," says Zion. "You just make sure they're not trying to forcibly get themselves out of the elevator. It's an inconvenience; you're stuck in a box. You'll just have to wait."

As part of his role, Zion also works on escalators, though he prefers elevators. "With escalators, at each end of that device is a little pit. And you have to crawl down in there." But he invests time in making sure whatever system he is working with runs at it's best. "We try to take on all aspects of it, from literally cleaning out the pit at the very bottom of the escalator from fire hazards and such to cleaning the car tops to re-roping them, modernizing the older elevators, changing them to newer equipment."

Elevators are complex machines with many different mechanical and electrical parts that must be constantly adjusted and maintained in order to work properly.

PREPARING YOURSELF

Becoming an elevator technician means going through an apprenticeship program with an elevator contractor company or a local trade union, which requires a high school diploma. It is helpful to take classes in shop, mechanical drawing, and math during high school, as apprentice elevator technician is a competitive field with few openings. Students usually have to apply for apprentice positions. Once accepted into a program, an apprentice must go through about four years of training, including 2,000 hours of paid work alongside an experienced technician for on-the-job training and 144 hours of classroom time. Classroom learning includes learning about safety, elevator and escalator parts, reading blueprints, electrical theory, and electronics. Once an apprentice has finished the program, they are fully qualified as elevator mechanics or assistant mechanics.

Some states also require elevator techs to be licensed, which means taking a state exam. There are also certificate programs available from the National Association of Elevator Contractors, which grant certificates as a certified elevator technician or a certified accessibility and private residence lift technician. Some techs also attend college to get a two-year associate's degree in electronics. No matter whether they pursue certification or not, techs are expected to continue learning throughout their career, to keep up with new technological developments in elevators and other equipment.

FUTURE PROSPECTS

Elevator technicians are in demand because of the growth in the construction of office buildings and stores that need elevators and escalators. Providing access for disabled people in public buildings is also an increasing need because of new government regulations concerning handicapped access. There is a continuing need to repair and update old elevators, as well as install new and more sophisticated controls and electronics. All of these factors contribute to an estimated 13 percent increase in elevator tech jobs over the next ten years, a faster than average rate of growth than all other jobs. However, elevator techs have a fairly high hourly wage, which makes these jobs very competitive.

FOR MORE INFORMATION

BOOKS

Bernard, Andreas. *Lifted: A Cultural History of the Elevator*. New York, NY: NYU Press, 2014.
This book talks about the invention and history of elevators and how they changed modern life.

Brain, Marshall. *The Engineering Book: From the Catapult to the Curiosity Rover, 250 Milestones in the History of Engineering*. New York, NY: Sterling Publishing, 2015.
This book looks at twenty-five milestones in engineering, including the invention of the elevator.

McCain, Zach. *Elevators 101*. 3rd ed. Mobile, AL: Elevator Books, 2015.
Written by an engineer and certified elevator safety inspector, this book is a basic introduction to elevators and how they work and is especially useful for people who need just a general knowledge of elevators.

Strakosch, G.R. *Sam & Samantha, The Mainteneers*. Mobile, AL: Elevator Books, 2015.

This is a fictional account of what elevator maintenance technicians might encounter in a day on the job.

ORGANIZATIONS

International Union of Elevator Constructors
7154 Columbia Gateway Drive
Columbia, MD 21046
Website: https://www.iuec.org
This trade union represents elevator technicians and also offers apprenticeship information.

National Association of Elevator Contractors
1298 Wellbrook Circle
Conyers, GA 30012
(800) 900-6232
Website: http://naec.org
This association represents the elevator industry, including independent contractors and equipment manufacturers.

PERIODICALS

Elevator World
354 Morgan Avenue
PO Box 6507
Mobile, AL 36660
(251) 479-4514
Website: http://www.elevatorworld.com
This magazine, intended for people in the elevator
industry, has articles about elevator technology,
elevator contracting, current news, and related topics.
It also has similar editions published in other regions
including India, the Middle East, and Latin America.

BLOG

Elevator World Unplugged
Website: http://www.elevatorworld.com/blogs
This blog includes posts that are sometimes funny,
but also contain information about research
and education.

VIDEO

"IUEC More Than a Job"
Website: https://www.youtube.com/
watch?v=DR512Hn89SA&nohtml5=False
Members of the International Union of Elevator
Constructors discuss the opportunities and training
available through their union and how it is a career,
not just a job.

"IUEC New York City Apprenticeship Feature"
Website: https://www.youtube.com/
watch?v=ymgY0uQ0Y-0&nohtml5=False
Created by the International Union of Elevator
Constructors, this video talks about the basics of
elevator technology and the process of becoming an
apprentice in the field.

WEBSITES

Due to the changing nature of internet links, Rosen Publishing has developed an online list of websites related to the subject of this book. This site is updated regularly. Please use this link to access the list:

http://www.rosenlinks.com/CCWC/repair

CHAPTER 7

LINE WORKER

There's a major storm, like a blizzard or a hurricane or an ice storm. Power is knocked out and the electrical lines are down. Who is the hero when towns and cities are in this situation? Often it's line workers, who work for an electrical or telecommunications utility. They use their trucks and buckets to reach and repair broken electrical wires or transformers and restore power, heat, and lights.

"Line worker" is the term used to describe line installers and repairers. They install and repair electrical power systems and telecommunications cables, including fiber optic cables. Those who work for an electrical utility are basically installing and maintaining the power grid, which is the network of power lines and towers that connect homes and businesses to the sources of electricity. They can work locally, or they can be part of a crew that travels from state to state to repair and maintain interstate power lines and towers that run across long distances. Telecommunications line workers usually work locally,

Electric power lines often need repair, especially in the aftermath of a large storm or other natural disaster.

installing and repairing the many different kinds of cables used by telephone, television, and internet providers. In both kinds of utilities, line workers may specialize either in installation or in repair. In the event of a major disaster in another part of the country, a line worker may travel to another area for a period of time to help restore power. Line workers need to be available at all times in case of emergency, so there will be times when they are on call and must go out and work in the middle of the night or on weekends and holidays.

Line workers are generally physically fit, because they have to climb and carry heavy equipment. Since much of the repair work is done from a ladder or in the bucket of a utility truck high above the ground, tolerance for heights is a must. Safety gear is essential, including harnesses and hardhats, as well as insulated work gloves and clothing to protect workers from live wires. Work is always done outside, no matter what the weather is, and emergency situations may mean working in some of the worst weather, such as snow, ice, rain, or high winds. It can also be a dangerous job, since line workers work around live high-voltage power lines.

Line workers are usually required to climb tall utility poles or ride in mechanical buckets that lift them high into the air. It is best if they aren't afraid of heights!

A DAY IN THE LIFE OF A LINE WORKER

Line workers share some tasks, whether they work for a local electrical utility or for a cable television company. Electrical line workers workday can include these tasks:

- Install, maintain, or repair the power lines that move electricity
- Inspect and identify defective devices, voltage regulators, transformers, and switches
- Climb poles and transmission towers and use truck-mounted buckets to get to equipment
- Operate power equipment when installing and repairing poles, towers, and lines
- Follow safety standards and procedures

Telecommunications line workers have some different tasks, especially since some installations take place underground:

- Install, maintain, inspect, and repair telecommunications equipment and lines
- Lay underground cable, including fiber optic lines, directly in trenches
- Pull cables in underground conduit
- Install aerial cables, including over lakes or across rivers

Line workers don't always work on utility poles. Sometimes they dig trenches and work on underground utility lines.

ON THE JOB

David Weaver is an electrical line worker in Texas. He answered some questions for Energy.gov about his job:

How did you end up in your career?

I have always enjoyed working outside, working with my hands and working with other people. When I was younger, a transformer needed to be changed out a couple houses down from me. I was in the backyard when the crew came to change it out. The crew leader explained the whole process as the lineman climbed the pole and proceeded to change the transformer. I was hooked after that.

What is the best part of working in your field?

The best part is that there is a lot of variety, and while all jobs do have a sense of similarity, no job is the same. I love being outside and — since I never have been one to see myself sitting behind a desk — this job fits me very well. You also meet so many different people, and the people you work with — whether you get along with them or not — become like a family.

PREPARING YOURSELF

Becoming a line worker first requires a high school diploma. During high school, it is also helpful to take classes in algebra and trigonometry. Some students earn degrees or certificates in electricity and electronics from a community college, but they are not required. Line workers receive extensive paid on-the-job training from their employers or from labor unions, which can—but doesn't always—mean enrolling in an apprenticeship program. Many electrical utility companies have training facilities with utility poles and large equipment, where apprentices can learn how to climb and how to work on things like transformers. Once line workers have completed an apprentice program, they become journeymen line workers and can work without supervision. They can also eventually advance to being supervisors or trainers. A commercial driver's license (CDL) is also required for workers who will be driving large utility trucks. Workers must get these from their state's department of motor vehicles.

FUTURE PROSPECTS

Line worker jobs are expected to grow at about the same rate as all other jobs, around 6 percent over the coming ten years, but jobs for electrical line workers will grow faster than telecommunications. Every new construction project as cities and towns expand will require new power lines and electrical service. There is also more repair and maintenance work to be done with electrical lines. Telecommunications will not grow as quickly because many households already have high-speed internet and cable, and they are sometimes seen as luxuries, not necessities. Workers who have already completed their apprenticeships or have two-year degrees will find the most jobs open to them.

FOR MORE INFORMATION

BOOKS

Herman, Stephen. *Delmar's Standard Textbook of Electricity*. 6th ed. Farmington Hills, MI: Cengage Learning, 2015.
Written by a retired engineer with experience in electricity, this is a practical how-to book of basic electric theory and practical applications, intended for students training to become electricians.

Parker, Steve. *DK Eyewitness Books: Electricity*. New York, NY: DK Publishing, 2013.
This book, written for young readers, is a highly visual introduction to electricity, its discovery, and how it works and is distributed.

Van Soelen, Wayne. *The Guidebook for Linemen and Cablemen*. 2nd ed. Farmington Hills, MI: Cengage Learning, 2011.
This reference book is for people actively training to become line workers, and covers topics such as working in environments and situations that line workers most often face, as well as equipment and safety.

PERIODICALS

Safety+Health
National Safety Council
1121 Spring Lake Drive
Itasca, IL 60143
(800) 621-7619
Website: http://www.safetyandhealthmagazine.com
The official magazine of the National Safety Council,
  this safety magazine often includes articles for
  line workers and other utility workers about safety
  conditions and hazards on the job.

Utility Worker
Utility Workers Union of America
1300 L Street NW, #1200
Washington, DC 20005
(202) 899-2851
Website: http://uwua.net/utility-worker-magazine
Published by the Utility Workers Union of America, this
  is the official magazine for the utility worker's trade
  union, including industry news, job information,
  and technology.

ORGANIZATIONS

Edison Electric Institute (EEI)
701 Pennsylvania Avenue NW
Washington, DC 20004-2696
202-508-5000
Website: http://www.eei.org
EEI represents all US-owned electric utilities and the
people who work for those companies.

International Brotherhood of Electrical Workers (IBEW)
900 Seventh Street NW
Washington, DC 20001
(202) 833-7000
Website: http://www.ibew.org
The IBEW is a trade union that represents people who
work in a wide variety of fields, including utilities,
construction, telecommunications, broadcasting,
manufacturing, railroads, and government. They also
publish an online magazine called the *Electrical Worker*.

VIDEOS

"A Day in the Life of a Lineworker"
Website: https://www.youtube.com/
    watch?v=8MTqHC5ba-k&nohtml5=False
This video is a good overview of how electrical power is
    created and gets to homes and what the career of a
    line worker is like.

"Get Energized: Journeyman Line Worker Career"
Website: https://www.youtube.com/
    watch?v=DlQ7gyS0iW0
This short video showcases the job of a journey line
    worker in the electric utility industry.

WEBSITES

Due to the changing nature of internet links, Rosen
Publishing has developed an online list of websites
related to the subject of this book. This site is updated
regularly. Please use this link to access the list:

http://www.rosenlinks.com/CCWC/repair

CHAPTER 8

MASONRY WORKER

For someone who likes to fix things, there are options beyond mechanics and technicians. Masons are craftsmen who work with stone, brick, and other types of masonry, either building with those materials or repairing things made from them. A mason might build a stone wall, repair a foundation, or lay a brick walkway. Masonry is one of the oldest professions in the world, going back to ancient times and the construction of some of the oldest buildings in the world. Stonemasons use both hand and power tools to shape stone and other materials into custom shapes to fit buildings, memorials, or other stone objects.

The overall term "mason" refers to several different types of jobs working with real or artificial materials. Brick masons, block masons, and bricklayers use bricks, blocks, and masonry panels to construct and maintain walls, fireplaces, walkways, and the exteriors of buildings. A stonemason uses natural stone, such as granite or marble, or manmade stones of concrete to build fences, walkways, floors, walls, and

While some masons work on constructing new buildings, others repair existing structures, such as this brick wall.

landscaping features. Stonemasons may also be employed in restoration work on old buildings and other structures, replacing damaged or missing decorative or structural pieces. Some stonemasons specialize in memorials like tombstones and commemorative stone tablets. There are also cement masons and concrete finishers, who work with concrete to create walls and sidewalks or structural elements like beams, columns, and panels.

Masonry work takes skill and attention to detail. Stone masons often use very detailed blueprints that number each stone that is going into a specific project, using special hammers, chisels, and diamond-bladed saws to cut through stone and shape it correctly. Stonemasons building a wall may build it using mortar to keep the stones together or dry-fit them so that they don't require mortar. They must balance and fit the stones together and keep the wall from collapsing. Bricklayers not only lay rows, or courses, of brick using mortar to hold them together, but they also have to trim bricks when necessary to fit the size of the structure. They must make sure that a brick wall stays straight as it builds upwards. They may use an arch of brick around window openings. Bricklayers might also work on older brick buildings, repairing walls by repointing (putting in new mortar) the existing bricks and replacing any that are damaged or missing.

Most masons work for a contractor who specializes in certain types of masonry. Some are also self-employed. Most masonry jobs involve being outside, standing, kneeling, and bending for long periods of time in areas that are often muddy or dirty. It is also a strenuous job, requiring the lifting of heavy stone. Masons risk cuts by the tools they use to cut and shape stone. They can also be injured by falls from scaffolds, particularly if employed in building chimneys.

A DAY IN THE LIFE OF A STONE MASON

Most stonemasons work forty hours a week, but during construction season, when the weather is warmer and most building activity is taking place, they may be working longer weeks, compensated by slower weeks in the winter. A stone mason may:

- Read blueprints or drawings to calculate materials needed for construction
- Lay out patterns, forms, materials, and foundations according to plans
- Mix mortar or grout and spread it onto a slab or foundation
- Clean and polish surfaces with hand or power tools

There is a customer service element as well, particularly for stonemasons who do residential work such as landscaping structures or those who carve memorials. They must be good at working with and listening to the needs and wants of their customers.

PREPARING YOURSELF

Working as a stonemason requires a high school diploma. During high school, classes in mechanical drawing and

A stone mason has a specialized set of equiptment for his or her work. Masons often use power tools such as saws to cut through old stone or brick or to shape new pieces for building.

math are helpful, as well as any vocational construction classes. Some masons do attend a technical school to get a degree or certificate in masonry, but most learn on the job through apprenticeship programs. A masonry contractor or labor union usually sponsors apprenticeship programs. An apprenticeship lasts three to four years and takes place under the supervision of a journeyman or master level mason. It includes 2,000 hours of paid training on the job and at least 144 hours of related classroom training. On-the-job training begins with minor assisting tasks, and in classroom training, apprentices learn construction basics such as blueprint reading; mathematics, including measurement, volume, and mixing proportions; building code requirements; and safety and first-aid practices.

FUTURE PROSPECTS

Stonemasons and bricklayers are expected to see as much as a 19 percent increase in job opportunities in the next ten years, which is a much faster rate than the average for all other occupations. The number of jobs can depend on the number of new construction projects underway, but with an increasing population, the number of municipal buildings like schools and hospitals will increase, and they

A DIFFERENT KIND OF MASONRY

Harriet Pace is a stonemason in England, but she isn't building stone walls or brick paths. As part of her apprenticeship, she is working on the restoration of York Cathedral in York, England, the largest Gothic cathedral in Europe. Harriet describes her work on My Job Search:

> A usual day's work includes using a mallet and chisel to shape stone to the original cathedral features, fixing the stone into the building and occasionally doing mortar repairs on weathered stone. It is a building of such beauty and magnitude that you can't help but fall in love with your job. Not only are you making history, you're also helping to conserve it. I've always been a creative and imaginative person who loves art and design and architecture and it's like all those things rolled into one. And what makes stone masonry so special, besides the stunning buildings you're working on, is that learning a new craft is never-ending and that makes every day both interesting and challenging.

require masons for their construction. Brick continues to be a popular building material as well, and older brick buildings always need maintenance and repair. Concrete masons will be in demand for roads, bridges, and other structures, since concrete is weatherproof and strong. It is also being used more and more for hurricane-proof buildings, also increasing the demand for good concrete masons and finishers.

Masonry requires strength for lifting large blocks of stone, even with the help of machines such as this pulley system. The materials involved are so heavy that they often require a few people to manage.

FOR MORE INFORMATION

BOOKS

Cramb, Ian. *The Art of the Stonemason*. Chambersburg, PA: Alan C. Hood & Company, 2006.
This book gives the principles of the stonemason's art, told by a mason who grew up in a family tradition of stonemasonry.

Ham, Robert Benjamin. *Residential Construction Academy: Masonry, Brick and Block Construction*. Clifton Park, NY: Delmar Cengage Learning, 2007.
This book introduces and explains modern residential masonry construction procedures, as well as current building and construction industry safety regulations.

Kicklighter, Clois E., and Timothy L. Andera. *Modern Masonry: Brick, Block, Stone*. 8th ed. Tinley Park, IL: Goodheart-Willcox, 2015.
This book covers everything about working with brick, block, stone, and concrete, as well as building codes and safety issues.

ORGANIZATIONS

International Masonry Institute (IMI)
17101 Science Drive

Bowie, MD 20715

(800) 803-0295

Website: http://imiweb.org

The IMI is an alliance between the International Union of Bricklayers and contractors who employ them, offering education, technical support, research, and training.

International Union of Bricklayers and Allied Craftworkers (BAC)

620 F Street NW

Washington, DC 20004

(888) 880-8222

Website: http://www.bacweb.org

The BAC represents craftworkers in the trowel trades across the United States and Canada, including bricklayers, stone and marble masons, cement masons, plasterers, tile setters, terrazzo and mosaic workers, and pointers/cleaners/caulkers.

PERIODICALS

Masonry

Mason Contractors Association of America

33 South Roselle Road
Schaumburg, IL 60193
(800) 536-2225
Website: http://www.masonrymagazine.com
This is the official magazine of the Mason Contractors
 Association of America and has articles about
 the craft of stonemasonry as well as the practical
 business side.

VIDEOS

"Career in Stonemasonry"
Website: https://www.youtube.com/watch?v=h0C5f-
 NFcro&nohtml5=False
This video shows three aspiring masons in England
 as they learn the basics of the craft, from quarrying
 stone to carving, under the mentorship of an
 experienced stonemason.

"Learning Stonemasonry in Britain"
Website: https://www.youtube.com/
 watch?v=Xd2AprD7sRM
An aspiring stonemason in England spends a day with
 a local stonemasonry company learning about what
 they do.

BLOGS

Living Stone Masonry
Website: http://www.livingstonemasons.com/blog
This blog is written by Franklin Smith, owner of Living
    Stone Masonry, and includes posts about repair jobs
    his company is doing, as well as techniques and
    services

The Path to Stonemasonry
Website: http://www.lovellstonegroup.com/news/blog-
    the-path-to-stonemasonry/
Sponsored by the Lovell Stone Group quarry masters
    and masons, this blog discusses what it's like to work in
    stonemasonry and what it takes to learn the craft.

WEBSITES

Due to the changing nature of internet links, Rosen
Publishing has developed an online list of websites
related to the subject of this book. This site is updated
regularly. Please use this link to access the list:

http://www.rosenlinks.com/CCWC/repair

CHAPTER 9

NUCLEAR POWER PLANT TECHNICIAN

A nuclear power plant, which generates electricity from nuclear reactions, is a complex place to work. To actually run the nuclear reactor requires education and licensing from the government and other organizations. But there are jobs within nuclear power plants that don't require college degrees or certifications to get started and can pay well, such as a nuclear power mechanic or technician. Generally, a mechanic or technician in a power plant assists other professionals, such as reactor operators, engineers, and scientists, in the work of running the power plant.

Nuclear power plants and research facilities are controlled by complex machinery and systems in control rooms like this. The systems require constant monitoring and maintenance by skilled technicians.

Many areas of a nuclear power facility require workers to wear protective clothing, to protect them from exposure to radiation.

A nuclear technician can be an operating technician or a radiation protection technician. Operating technicians perform corrective, preventative, and special maintenance on systems in the plant and its equipment to make sure it is working reliably and safely. They monitor the many systems that are required to make a plant run, such as the levels of contamination from radioactivity and other contaminants within the water system. Monitoring water levels can also help find any possible leaks and assure the plant's turbines, which generate the electricity, are working correctly and at full capacity. They measure pressure, temperature, and radiation levels and make adjustments and repairs when necessary.

Radiation protection technicians are concerned with protecting people from radiation contamination, both in the plant and in the surrounding area. They use radiation detectors to measure levels in the plant and other areas and a piece of equipment called a dosimeter to measure radiation in people and objects. They go out into the area around a power plant and take air and plant samples, as well as samples of milk from cows grazing in the vicinity. They may also work on radiation protection plans and procedures, as well as alerting personnel if they are entering a high dose area or working in an unsafe manner.

Nuclear plant techs may also work in the waste management areas of the power plant, monitoring the disposal, recycling, and storage of nuclear waste and contaminated materials such as protective clothing and rags.

A tech needs to be able to inspect and troubleshoot different types of valves, pumps, and other equipment and repair them if necessary. They also need to be able to work within a team with other work groups and maintenance personnel, since job assignments may require more than one person to complete them. A tech may work in an office or control room or in other areas of the plant or outside. They may need to wear protective clothing when going into areas of high radiation.

A DAY IN THE LIFE OF A NUCLEAR TECH

The tasks that a nuclear technician does in a typical day will vary according to what part of plant operations they are concerned with. But they may include:

- Monitor the equipment used in nuclear experiments and power generation
- Measure the levels and types of radiation produced by nuclear experiments, power generation, and other activities
- Collect samples of air, water, and soil and test for radioactive contamination
- Instruct personnel on radiation safety procedures and warn of hazardous conditions
- Operate and maintain radiation monitoring equipment

Normally, technicians work a forty hour week, but since nuclear power plants operate continuously, they will usually work rotating shifts, which means they may work days for a period of time, then afternoons, and then overnight. During refueling outages, when the power plant exchanges old nuclear fuel rods for fresh ones, techs may be working much more than forty hours a week over several months.

Nuclear power plant technicians often need to take samples of water, air, and even cow's milk from areas surrounding the plant, to make sure that no contamination is taking place.

ROBOTS AND PROTECTIVE GEAR

Interviewed by Duke Energy, Keith Ferdinando spoke about his role as a radiation protection tech at a nuclear plant in 2013. His responsibilities include helping limit site teammates' radiological exposure, or, as they call it, "dose". He uses his knowledge and equipment to help locate it, as well as brainstorm ways to reduce employees' exposure.

On an average day, Ferdinando logs on to his remote radiological monitoring system. He explains, "We have remote monitors throughout the site's radiological areas which ensure radiological levels stay normal. These machines are extremely helpful because not only will they alert us if the radiation level exceeds a specific set point, but they also let us know the radiation level of an area before we go in." Technicians rely on these technologies to reduce radiation exposure; Ferdinando's most recent tool is a mobile robot with cameras and a gripper arm, to go into areas with high radiation levels and extreme conditions. The robot can even climb stairs! Instead of sending a teammate into those areas, he can send iRobot in to do the dangerous job of manual examinations and testing.

PREPARING YOURSELF

Most nuclear technicians learn on the job, although some nuclear plants prefer people who have a two-year college degree in nuclear science or nuclear technology. A high school diploma is required. Many plants also prefer people with some experience, especially those who served in the US Navy and have nuclear experience from the navy's nuclear power schools. High school classes in mathematics, physics, and chemistry are also useful. Nuclear power plant employees must also pass extensive background and security checks with the government as well as their employer. Techs learn under the supervision of experienced personnel, attending classroom training, often onsite at the plant. Training programs last from six months to two years, after which techs can work unsupervised, but they will continue to go through training throughout their careers to stay current with procedures and technology.

FUTURE PROSPECTS

Employment opportunities in nuclear power are expected to decline in the next ten years, mostly because of the fact that many nuclear power plants will reach the end of their licensed life span and will be closed down. Other technologies in energy generation are gaining popularity, but nuclear power may gain traction as a replacement for fossil fuel energy sources. Even without operating power plants, techs will be needed to maintain and repair the storage facilities for spent nuclear fuel. Nuclear techs will also continue to be needed in the military and defense industries.

FOR MORE INFORMATION

BOOKS

Ferguson, Charles D. *Nuclear Energy: What Everyone Needs to Know*. New York, NY; Oxford University Press, 2011.
Written for all readers and not just those in the nuclear industry, this book is an overview of nuclear energy, how it works, its safety, and what the future might bring.

Hansen, Amy S. *Nuclear Energy: Amazing Atoms*. New York, NY: Rosen Publishing, 2010.
This book, written for young readers, explains how nuclear power works and how it generates electricity.

Lusted, Marcia Amidon. *Innovative Technologies: Nuclear Energy*. Minneapolis, MN: Abdo Publishing, 2013.
This is an overview for young readers interested in nuclear energy and how the different types of power plants work.

ORGANIZATIONS

Nuclear Energy Institute (NEI)
1201 F Street NW, Suite 1100
Washington, DC 20004-1218
(202) 739-8000
Website: http://www.nei.org

NEI's mission is to promote the peaceful uses of nuclear energy and its global importance. It reaches out both to those in the nuclear industry and those who want to know more about nuclear power with news, industry issues, and educational materials.

World Nuclear Association
Tower House
10 Southampton Street
London WC2E 7HA
England
+44 (0)20 7451 1520
Website: http://www.world-nuclear.org
The World Nuclear Association's mission is to create a wider understanding of nuclear energy around the world. It provides news, training and educational materials, basic information, and industry support

PERIODICALS

Nuclear Plant Journal
1400 Opus Place, Suite 904
Downers Grove, IL 60515
(630) 858 6161

Website: http://nuclearplantjournal.com
Nuclear Plant Journal provides technical information for people working in the nuclear power industry and promotes research and development for safe and peaceful uses of nuclear power around the world.

VIDEOS

"How Nuclear Energy Works"
Website: https://www.youtube.com/watch?v=VJfIbBDR3e8
This video explains the basics of nuclear power and addresses some of the controversies surrounding it.

"Nuclear Energy Explained: How does it work?"
Website: https://www.youtube.com/watch?v=rcOFV4y5z8c
Produced by PBS, this video takes the viewer on a tour of a nuclear power plant under construction.

"Nuclear Power"
Website: http://www.pbs.org/video/2220837749/
This video takes the viewer inside a nuclear power plant to explain how nuclear energy becomes electricity.

WEBSITES

Due to the changing nature of internet links, Rosen Publishing has developed an online list of websites related to the subject of this book. This site is updated regularly. Please use this link to access the list:

http://www.rosenlinks.com/CCWC/repair

CHAPTER 10

SMALL ENGINE REPAIR MECHANIC

For some people, the perfect career is one with flexibility, such as being able to work when they want to and be their own boss. For someone who loves to fix things, one of the best careers in this category is to be a small engine repair mechanic. While some small engine mechanics work for other companies, many operate their own businesses, often out of their own homes and garages.

A small engine repair mechanic works on things like lawnmowers, motorcycles, snow blowers, snowmobiles, portable generators, and motorboat engines. They might even specialize in outdoor equipment like mowers, trimmers, and chain saws or repair anything with a small engine. They troubleshoot problems and make repairs, as well as doing routine maintenance. They inspect and test parts and replace anything worn or broken. They might have to drain old fuel and replace carburetors or sharpen dull blades or work with mechanical, electrical, and fuel problems. Sometimes a repair is small, but other times it might require disassembling an

Small engines can require a great deal of hands-on repair of vital parts, like tightening spark plugs.

entire engine and then putting it back together. Small engine mechanics may use just hand tools, or they may have access to computerized troubleshooting systems and power tools, depending on where they work.

Small engine repair mechanics may work in their own shops, running their own business, and perhaps combining it with sales of small power equipment. Others might work for a larger repair company. Some mechanics work in the tool rental and repair departments of large home improvement stores or rental stores. If a mechanic specializes in small boat engines, he or she may work at a marina, or if working on their own, have to travel to boat storage areas and docks.

A DAY IN THE LIFE OF A SMALL ENGINE MECHANIC

The daily tasks of a small engine repair mechanic might differ slightly depending on what kind of equipment is worked on and whether they run their own business or work for a larger company. But, mechanics could:

- Discuss equipment issues, maintenance plans, and work performed with customers
- Perform routine engine maintenance, such as lubricating parts or replacing spark plugs
- Test and inspect engines for malfunctioning parts
- Repair or replace worn, defective, or broken parts

Many small engine mechanics specialize in repairing machinery such as snowmobiles or motorcycles.

- Reassemble and reinstall components and engines following repairs
- Keep records of inspections, test results, work performed, and parts used
- Send invoices for work done and keep records of payments

A mechanic working for a rental company or home improvement store may also have to stay current with store policies and promotions and participate in employee activities in other parts of the store, such as sales or customer service. Repair shops can be noisy and sometimes dirty environments. Some mechanics make service calls to homes and businesses and may have to work outside in bad weather.

PREPARING YOURSELF

Most small engine repair mechanics have high school diplomas. Many high schools have vocational classes in small engine repair, metal fabrication, and auto mechanics. Some mechanics may also earn two-year degrees from a vocational training school or community college, especially if they plan to work for a larger company or need training in more sophisticated types of repair. Motorcycle mechanics often have secondary training because employers prefer to hire people with specialized knowledge. Such mechanics will also need a motorcycle operator's license.

Most mechanics receive their training on the job from a more experienced mechanic. Sometimes an employer will send a mechanic to a training course offered by a particular manufacturer or on a specific product. Many motorcycle and motorboat manufacturers also offer certification in repairing their own specific models. Mechanics can also earn a certificate from the Equipment and Engine Training Council, which can be helpful when looking for employment.

Lawn mowers are machines that almost every homeowner needs, but many do not understand the mechanics of how they work.

FUTURE PROSPECTS

The job outlook for small engine repair mechanics is a little slower than the average for all other jobs, at about a 4 percent expected growth rate, according to the Bureau of Labor Statistics. However, motorcycles are increasing in popularity,

A GROWING SHORTAGE

In some parts of the country, there is actually a shortage of small engine repair mechanics. At certain times of year especially, such as spring (for lawn care machinery) and fall (for snow blowers), customers might have to wait weeks for repairs. Some shops even have computerized courses to teach small engine repair to employees without experience, but still can't get the help they need. Al Painter, a repair shop owner in Florida, discusses the difficulties he has finding enough help in *Clay Today*:

> Because there is a great need for small engine mechanics, Painter hopes that high school graduates seeking a path other than college will consider his line of work. "Everybody can't go to college," Painter said. "Everybody doesn't want to go to college. And half the people that go to college don't know what they want to do when they get out of college. A lot of people like to work with their hands." Without small engine mechanics, replacing equipment such as lawn mowers, trimmers, pumps and generators would be costly. "If you have a $1,000 lawn mower, it may take $200 to fix or you can replace it for $1,000, but you're not going to chunk it," Painter said. "In the old days, you could replace them, but the good lawn mowers are going to cost you about $2,000." Because there is a great need for small engine mechanics, Painter hopes that high school graduates seeking a path other than college will consider his line of work.

Many small engine repair mechanics receive their first training at the high school level. Others attend trade schools and learn about small engines there.

so there will be a need for skilled motorcycle mechanics. And because many types of engines, such as those in boats and outdoor power equipment, are getting more complex, many people can no longer work on their own equipment and will need a small engine repair mechanic to keep their machines running. There will be more competition for jobs among mechanics that have no education or certification beyond a high school diploma.

FOR MORE INFORMATION

BOOKS

Demspey, Paul. *Small Gas Engine Repair*. New York, NY: McGraw-Hill, 2008.
This book, written by a master mechanic, is a step-by-step hands-on guide to repairing small gasoline engines.

Demspey, Paul. *Two Stroke Engine Repair and Maintenance*. New York, NY: McGraw-Hill, 2009.
This guide covers repairing small two-stroke engines, which are found in many kinds of lawn and home equipment.

Hunn, Peter. *Small Engines and Outdoor Power Equipment: A Care & Repair Guide for: Lawn Mowers, Snowblowers & Small Gas-Powered Implements*. Minneapolis, MN: Cool Springs Press, 2014.
This book is a how-to manual written for the homeowner, for repairing many types of small engines that are routinely used around the house. It includes both basic and more complicated repairs.

ORGANIZATIONS

Association of Marine Technicians (AMTECH)
Education Division:
513 River Estates Parkway
Canton, GA 30115-3019
(800) 467-0982
Website: http://www.am-tech.org
AMTECH is dedicated to promoting excellence
among technicians who service marine engines
and equipment.

Equipment & Engine Training Council
3880 Press Wallace Drive
York, SC 29745
(888) 406-1810
Website: http://www.eetc.org
This nonprofit council was established to deal with
the shortage of qualified outdoor power equipment
mechanics and to provide education and training
opportunities.

PERIODICALS

Engine Builder
Babcox Media, Inc.
3550 Embassy Parkway
Akron, OH 44333
(330) 670-1234
Website: http://www.enginebuildermag.com
This magazine is for engine mechanics, with articles that address both small engines and automotive engines.

VIDEOS

"Small Engine Mechanic"
https://www.youtube.com/watch?v=uWstbftOtp8&nohtml5=False
Part of the "Try it for 5" series for career information, this short video shows what it is like to be a small engine mechanic.

"Small Engine Mechanic Careers Overview"
Website: https://www.youtube.com/watch?v=qpxQaf4tNGQ

Intended for anyone who is interested in repairing small engines for a living, this video shows the daily working life of a small engine mechanic.

"Tools of the Small Engine Mechanic"
Website: https://www.youtube.com/
watch?v=0b7XfJJ6KcI&nohtml5=False
This video is intended for educators and students to learn about the basic tools of a small engine mechanic.

WEBSITES

Due to the changing nature of internet links, Rosen Publishing has developed an online list of websites related to the subject of this book. This site is updated regularly. Please use this link to access the list:

http://www.rosenlinks.com/CCWC/repair

GLOSSARY

APPRENTICE A person who is learning a trade from a skilled employer, usually at a low wage for a certain period of time.

APTITUDE The natural ability to do something well.

AVIATION The design, development, production, and operation of airplanes.

BEARINGS The part of a machine that is supporting another part when it turns.

BLUEPRINT A design plan or technical drawing for making or building something.

BOILER A tank that creates steam under pressure, to power a steam engine.

CODES A set of laws or regulations for safety or building specifications.

DEXTERITY Skill, ease, and the ability to perform tasks with the hands.

DIAGNOSTIC A practice or tool used to help identify a problem or malfunction.

DUCTS A channel or tube for moving things like water or air.

GAUGE An instrument or device with a visual display, which measures amount or content.

HYDRAULIC A system that is operated or moved using a fluid.

MECHANICAL Something that is produced or operated by a machine or tool.

MONOMETER An instrument used for measuring the pressure of liquids or gases.

PHOTOVOLTAIC A method of generating electrical power using solar energy.

PHYSICS The branch of science concerning the nature and properties of matter and energy.

RIGGING The ropes, wires, or other structures built to support people or equipment.

SCREENING Examining people for things such as evidence of drug use, in order to decide if they are suitable for a certain job or purpose.

SPECIFICATIONS A standard of workmanship or materials that must be met when making or fixing something.

VOCATIONAL Education or training specifically related to occupations or employment.

BIBLIOGRAPHY

"Aircraft Mechanic (A&P) Jobs." Avjobs. Accessed April 7, 2016 (http://www.avjobs.com/careers/detail.asp?Job_Title=Aircraft+Mechanic+%28A&P%29&Category=Airline&Related=Aviation+Maintenance&RecID=95).

"Basic Requirements to Become an Aircraft Mechanic." Federal Aviation Administration. Accessed April 7, 2016 (https://www.faa.gov/mechanics/become/basic).

"Becoming a Cruise Ship Diesel Mechanic." Diesel Mechanic Guide. Accessed April 7, 2016 (http://www.dieselmechanicguide.com/becoming-cruise-ship-diesel-mechanic).

Brick Mason, Block Mason and Stone Mason Career and Job Information. Career overview. Accessed April 10, 2016 (http://www.careeroverview.com/brick-mason-careers.html).

Bureau of Labor Statistics, U.S. Department of Labor. *Occupational Outlook Handbook, 2016-17 Edition*. Aircraft and Avionics Equipment Mechanics and Technicians. Accessed April 7, 2016 (http://www.bls.gov/ooh/installation-maintenance-and-repair/aircraft-and-avionics-equipment-mechanics-and-technicians.htm).

Bureau of Labor Statistics, U.S. Department of Labor. *Occupational Outlook Handbook, 2016-17 Edition*. Elevator Installers and Repairers. Accessed April 9, 2016 (http://www.bls.gov/ooh/construction-and-extraction/elevator-installers-and-repairers.htm).

Bureau of Labor Statistics, U.S. Department of Labor, *Occupational Outlook Handbook, 2016-17 Edition*. Heating, Air Conditioning, and Refrigeration Mechanics and Installers. Accessed April 8, 2016 (http://www.bls.gov/ooh/installation-maintenance-and-repair/heating-air-conditioning-and-refrigeration-mechanics-and-installers.htm).

Bureau of Labor Statistics, U.S. Department of Labor. *Occupational Outlook Handbook, 2016-17 Edition*. Line Installers and Repairers. Accessed April 9, 2016 (http://www.bls.gov/ooh/installation-maintenance-and-repair/line-installers-and-repairers.htm).

Bureau of Labor Statistics. U.S. Department of Labor, *Occupational Outlook Handbook, 2016-17 Edition*. Marine Engineers and Naval Architects (http://www.bls.gov/ooh/architecture-and-engineering/marine-engineers-and-naval-architects.htm).

Bureau of Labor Statistics, U.S. Department of Labor. *Occupational Outlook Handbook, 2016-17 Edition*,

Masonry Workers. Accessed April 10, 2016 (http://www.bls.gov/ooh/construction-and-extraction/brickmasons-blockmasons-and-stonemasons.htm).

Bureau of Labor Statistics, U.S. Department of Labor. *Occupational Outlook Handbook, 2016-17 Edition*. Nuclear Technicians. Accessed April 11, 2016 (http://www.bls.gov/ooh/life-physical-and-social-science/nuclear-technicians.htm).

Bureau of Labor Statistics, U.S. Department of Labor. *Occupational Outlook Handbook, 2016-17 Edition*. Plumbers, Pipefitters, and Steamfitters. Accessed April 7, 2016 (http://www.bls.gov/ooh/construction-and-extraction/plumbers-pipefitters-and-steamfitters.htm).

Bureau of Labor Statistics, U.S. Department of Labor. *Occupational Outlook Handbook, 2016-17 Edition*. Small Engine Mechanics. Accessed April 11, 2016 (http://www.bls.gov/ooh/installation-maintenance-and-repair/small-engine-mechanics.htm).

"A Candid Revelation of the Life of Junior Engineer Onboard a Ship." Bright Hub Engineering. Accessed April 7, 2016 (http://www.brighthubengineering.com/seafaring/25992-a-candid-revelation-of-the-life-of-junior-engineer-onboard-a-ship).

"Cruise Ship Mechanic Career Info." Study.com. Accessed April 7, 2016 (http://study.com/articles/Cruise_Ship_Mechanic_Information_About_a_Career_in_Cruise_Ship_Maintenance_and_Ship_Repair.html).

"A Day in the Life of a Radiation Protection Technician at Brunswick Nuclear Plant." Duke Energy, February 13, 2013 (https://nuclear.duke-energy.com/2013/02/13/a-day-in-the-life-of-a-radiation-protection-technician-at-brunswick-nuclear-plant).

"Elevator Installers and Repairers." Collegegrad.com. Accessed April 9, 2016 (https://collegegrad.com/careers/elevator-installers-and-repairers).

"Energy Jobs: Utility Line Worker." Energy.gov, November 19, 2014 (http://energy.gov/articles/energy-jobs-utility-line-worker).

"5 Hottest Smart Home Trends of 2015." HVAC Classes. Accessed April 8, 2016 (http://www.hvacclasses.org/blog/hottest-smart-home-trends-2015).

Graham, Ruth. "What It's Like To Be A Female Pipefitter." TheGrindstone.com, April 30, 2012 (http://www.thegrindstone.com/2012/04/30/mentors/what-its-like-to-be-a-female-pipefitter-461).

Hamilton, James. "Careers in Solar Power." US Department of Labor, Bureau of Labor Statistics.

Accessed April 8, 2016 (http://www.bls.gov/green/solar_power/#photovol).

"How a Smart House Works." Samsung. Accessed April 8, 2016 (http://techlife.samsung.com/smart-house-works-1017.html).

"HVAC Careers, Jobs and Training Information." Career Overview. Accessed April 8, 2016 (http://www.careeroverview.com/hvac-careers.html).

"Mechanical Technician." Nuclear Energy Institute. Accessed April 11, 2016 (http://www.nei.org/Careers-Education/Careers-in-the-Nuclear-Industry/Help-for-Your-Job-Search/Sample-Job-Descriptions-and-Salaries/Mechanical-Technician).

Rosser, Sarah Wakefield. "Small Engine Mechanic Shortage Coming?" *Clay Today*, December 3, 2015 (http://claytodayonline.com/stories/smallengine-mechanic-shortage-coming,341?).

"Small Engine Mechanics." Collegegrad.com. Accessed April 11, 2016 (https://collegegrad.com/careers/small-engine-mechanics).

Smith-Strickland, Kiona. "How Ships Survive a Hurricane at Sea." *Popular Mechanics*, June 5, 2014 (http://www.popularmechanics.com/adventure/outdoors/

tips/a10688/how-ships-survive-a-hurricane-at-sea-16862613).

"Solar Career Map." Interstate Renewable Energy Council. Accessed April 8, 2016 (http://irecsolarcareermap.org).

"Solar Career Map: Solar PV Installer." Interstate Renewable Energy Council. Accessed April 8, 2016 (http://irecsolarcareermap.org/jobs/solar-pv-installer).

"Solar Panel Installer Interview." MnEnergyCareers. Minnesota State Colleges and Universities, 2016 (https://www.iseek.org/industry/energy/careers/solar-panel-installer-interview.html).

"Solar Photovoltaic Installers." Collegegrad.com. Accessed April 8, 2016 (https://collegegrad.com/careers/solar-photovoltaic-installers).

"Steamfitter/Pipefitter/Sprinkler System Installer." Careers in Construction. Accessed April 7, 2016 (http://www.careersinconstruction.ca/en/career/steamfitterpipefittersprinkler-system-installer).

"Stonemason: What's it Really Like?" MyJobSearch.com. Accessed April 10, 2016 (http://myjobsearch.com/careers/stonemason.html).

Walzer, Philip, "At Work With: Alex Zion, Elevator Mechanic." *Virginian-Pilot*, March 5, 2012 (http://pilotonline.com/business/jobs/at-work-with-alex-zion-elevator-mechanic/article_c8ab551a-7c98-5137-8124-d7bfb5277d3c.html).

"What Does It Take to Become an Aircraft Mechanic?" Aviation Institute of Maintenance, August 25, 2014 (http://www.aviationmaintenance.edu/blog/aircraft-mechanic/take-become-aircraft-mechanic).

Zeigler, Matt. "Differences Between Steamfitters & Pipefitters." E-how. Accessed April 7, 2016 (http://www.ehow.com/list_7562435_differences-between-steamfitters-pipefitters.html).

INDEX

ABOUT THE AUTHOR

Marcia Amidon Lusted has written extensively for young readers. She is also an editor and writer for adults and also works in permaculture and sustainable design. She is actually pretty good at fixing things and recently learned how to wire and install electrical outlets. You can visit her at www.adventuresinnonfiction.com.

PHOTO CREDITS

Cover, p. 1 David Spates/Shutterstock.com; pp. 4–5 goodluz/Shutterstock.com; pp. 8–9 Westend61/Getty Images; pp. 11, 25 Thomas Barwick/Stone/Getty Images; p. 12 Orien Harvey/Lonely Planet Images/Getty Images; pp. 22–23 AlexRaths/iStock/Thinkstock; p. 26 BartCo/E+/Getty Images; pp. 34–35 Monty Rakusen/Cultura/Getty Images; p. 37 Chris Sattlberger/Cultura/Getty Images; p. 38 Hinterhaus Productions/Taxi/Getty Images; pp. 46–47 Lisa F. Young/Shutterstock.com; pp. 48, 76–77 Dmitry Kalinovsky/Shutterstock.com; p. 50 sturti/E+/Getty Images; pp. 58–59 Echo/Cultura/Getty Images; p. 60 goodluz/Shutterstock.com; p. 64 Randy Plett/The Image Bank/Getty Images; pp. 70–71 Jay P. Morgan/Photolibrary/Getty Images; pp. 72–73 © Agencja Fotograficzna Caro/Alamy Stock Photo; p. 85 Justin Sullivan/Getty Images; p. 87 Anthony Redpath/Corbis/Getty Images; p. 89 Mel Melcon/Los Angeles Times/Getty Images; p. 98 Morten Kjerulff/E+/Getty Images; p. 101 © iStockphoto.com/Elaine Odell; p. 103 Hakan Jansson/Maskot/Getty Images; pp. 110–111 Tiziana Fabi/AFP/Getty Images; p. 112 © BrazilPhotos.com/Alamy Stock Photo; p. 115 Alexis Orand/Gamma-Rapho/Getty Images; pp. 122–123 Portland Press Herald/Getty Images; p. 125 BanksPhotos/E+/Getty Images; p. 127 Hola Images/Getty Images; p. 129 Majority World/Universal Images Group/Getty Images; interior pages graphic (tools) Wiktoria Pawlak/Shutterstock.com.

Designer: Brian Garvey; Editor: Haley E. D. Houseman; Photo Researcher: Bruce Donnola.